*VIA* Folios 163

# Agrodolce

# Agrodolce

Poems by Luisa Maria Giulianetti

BORDIGHERA PRESS

All rights reserved. Parts of this book may be reprinted only by written permission from the author, and may not be reproduced for publication in book, magazine, or electronic media of any kind, except in quotations for purposes of literary reviews by critics.

© 2023, Luisa Maria Giulianetti

Library of Congress Control Number: 2023940206

Published by
BORDIGHERA PRESS
John D. Calandra Italian American Institute
25 W. 43rd Street, 17th Floor
New York, NY 10036

VIA Folios 163
ISBN 978-1-59954-197-6

# Table of Contents

| | |
|---|---|
| PREFACE | 13 |

## I. Passage

| | |
|---|---|
| Kneading | 19 |
| Serafina | 20 |
| Lezione: Brutta Figura | 22 |
| A Temporary Matter | 23 |
| Agrodolce | 24 |
| The Accidental Engineer | 28 |
| Rupture | 33 |
| Should I Not Survive the Year | 34 |
| Santi | 36 |
| The Pepper Jar | 37 |

## II. Dwelling

| | |
|---|---|
| What is Left | 41 |
| Lezione: In Cucina | 43 |
| Caesura | 44 |
| One of the Good Ones | 45 |
| Maria Reconceived | 47 |
| A Letter to Siena Maria | 50 |
| If These Trees Could Talk | 52 |
| Pasta con Finocchietto | 54 |
| Nonna's Pasta con Finocchietto | 56 |
| Beyond Blue | 58 |
| Mending World | 59 |

## III. Re-Membering

| | |
|---|---|
| Limone | 63 |
| Lezione: Sfortuna | 64 |
| Making Space | 65 |
| Salvation: A Blues | 67 |

| | |
|---|---|
| Sheltering with Sunflowers | 68 |
| Finding Home | 70 |
| Caponata | 72 |
| My family's Caponata | 73 |
| How to Drink Coffee Like an Italian: A Guide | 75 |
| Red, White, and Boiled | 76 |
| Within a World so Heavenly | 79 |
| Open Door | 80 |
| NOTES | 83 |
| ACKNOWLEDGEMENTS | 85 |
| ABOUT THE AUTHOR | 87 |

*For my parents*

*Chi si volta, e chi si gira,
sempre a casa va finire.*

No matter where you go or turn,
you will always end up at home.

**ITALIAN PROVERB**

This poem is a gesture toward
home, a request for passage
to the hillsides above Lucca,
Mount Etna's base, South
Brooklyn and North Chicago.
It moves among ghosts, lingers

in enameled pots and cast-iron
skillets. In the lees of the vinegar
jug. Helixed stories, strands
passed mother to daughter, before
the bleeding starts, as bread
rises. It resides in silences. Weighty.
In blue notes. On funeral cards.

This book raises the dead. Shakes
from their bones         tales
of grief and romance. Re-members
his spine arching the spike maul
hers bowed over a sewing machine.
        Palms clasped for the *tarantella*.
        Palms clasped in prayer.

On its back, it carries
the ruins I was willed. Starlight
gifted. I tend it     like I do
my daughter's labored breath
old-world seeds that vine
in my new world beds.

*agro* (sour) • *dolce* (sweet)

1. Italian for a sauce made by reducing sweet and sour elements. Its contrasting flavors are intense and well-balanced. A signature flavor in Sicilian cooking.

2. When grief and joy comingle. When the pang of loss is tempered by the sweetness of remembering.

# I. Passage

> Perhaps home is not a place but simply an irrevocable condition.
>
> JAMES BALDWIN, *GIOVANNI'S ROOM*

# Kneading

*Nonna Maria Grazia*

Burying three children and a young husband
shapes a woman, shrinks the world to a room.
Ghosts share space, hide in book spines.
She measures the survivors, their breaths

like handfuls of flour added to proofed yeast.
Kneading oxygen, she pushes supple dough,
pulls it in. Folds seams of memory and kin.
Scored loaves left to rise under baby quilts.

She washes bowls and scours pans.
Dresses baked bread with oil. Soup
awaits their arrival. Serving slow time
she bargains with saints for safe passage.

A century of waiting: dough to rise, doors
to open. Love knots what it cannot free.

# Serafina

The day your family left
for America, you were alone
for the first time. In the house
of your birth, where you birthed
and buried children. Stone-still
in widow's black.

You rose: to mix, knead
and proof. Forced to wed
the icy-eyed stranger you never
loved. To leave the boy you did.
When you broke it off, he cut
you, left you below the fig tree.

They say you never complained.
Loyal, ardent servant, caretaker
of fire, after the Seraphim, god's
watchful six-winged guardian
angels. Two wings hide their faces,
two cover their feet. A pair for flight.

Your swollen legs
throbbed against heavy wool
as you swept and dusted. Washed
scrubbed, wrung, dried. Pressed.
Tears mended. Tended the flame.
You never complained.

You ached sugar like tides ache
moon. Hid dried figs, *mostarda,
frutta martorana* in the suitcase
atop the armoire, unable to resist

their pull, even after you spiraled
into a near coma.

*Sei così debole.* He blamed
you for losing the boys—
the baby to measles, the older
to cancer. *Vecchia malvagia!*
Mocked your grief and failing
kidneys. You genuflected.

Yet, you taught Maria to bloom
yeast, bake loaves, candy orange
peel. To settle her stomach
with bay leaf. Weave Palm
Sunday fronds into crosses
to hang above her bed.

You'd trade the kingdom
for Seraphim wings, fan them wide
and soar. Snag a hidden sweet, cross
oceans. Return to the day
when his kiss, not his knife,
        blazed you.

# Lezione: Brutta Figura

*Non farci fare brutta figura!* Never arrive to someone's home empty-handed. Never bring *crisantemi*. They are the flowers of the dead. Dust daily: you never know who may come by. Do not leave the house with unironed clothes like Americans do. *Figurati!* When ironing, start from the back of the shirt. Use plenty of steam. Your clothes don't have to be new or fancy, but they must be clean and pressed. A little bleach and sunshine go a long way. Dryers ruin clothes. Place dried lavender in your closets and drawers. Things ironed stack neatly.

# A Temporary Matter

You returned, hungry
for things ripe and forgiving:
my bath-soft skin,
Empress plums.
I began spading
neglected soil, seeding
herbs and Sunday dinners.
Desire's amnesia.

You found your horn,
cleaned dulled rods, polished
bell and body satin.
You promised change
while folding shirts.
Played like the century
hadn't turned and Dexter
still packed the Keystone.

Before the leaves crimsoned
you were gone.

Jasmine cross-stitched
the gate, choked the latch.
In silence, heavy
like decay
I gather wilted plums
to shield winter injury.

On that last night
we found the Garrard
propped the screen
uncoiled the Miracles.
And we danced
beneath the moon's strobe.

# Agrodolce

> *Partenza: Porto di Palermo, 13 Ottobre 1946*
> *Arrival: Port of New York, 26 October 1946*
> *via SS Marine Shark*

I

She takes her first bite of America
from a yellow crescent fruit
at the Brooklyn table of *la famiglia
Chiaramonte*, who left *Caropepe*
soon after the war. The sweet
starchy flesh mellows
the sourness that has lodged
in her belly since Papà
announced, *a bruciapelo*,
that they would leave home
on a ship named Shark.
She ran to Nonna Fina and wept.

The adults drink wine, replay
the war: tanks, bombs, *i fascisti,
u tignusu*. Toast this new land
and promised work. She yearns
to fold into Nonna, into what
she's lost.

II

From the kitchen window
she tracks cars—so many cars—
rushing who knows where. A man
pushing a fruit cart disappears
around the corner. Iron ladders

zigzag down building
after grey building, linked
to the others by lines of hanging
clothing.　　　Swaying.

Will Mamma dry our clothes this way?
Are there fig trees to climb?


III

*Name?* Miss Mangano demands.
*Maria Manganaro*, she whispers.

They share a homeland and seven
surname letters. Yet *la maestra*
doesn't smile at her, never once
speaks a familiar word.

Maria can't mimic the odd *h* sound
American students make, wonders
why they swallow the ends of words.
Only numbers and equations ease
her drumming chest. She calculates
the minutes until Mamma will arrive.

*Name?*
*Maria . . .*
*Mary,* Miss Mangano corrects. *Mary.*


IV

The Shark heaved like a hungry
monster, ready to swallow her.
Pirates surely lie in wait. Eyes wide,
arms pinned to her sides, she

listened for Mamma's thin breath
from the bunk above.

Each morning, Mamma stroked
her matted curls, coaxed
her to eat. Bits of grapefruit,
stale and sour, bread that coated
her tongue metallic.
*Che brutto sapore.*
*Voglio pane di Nonna.*


V

In her dreams,
she crawls within the thick
arms of the old fig.


VI

She hasn't seen a single fig tree
in Brooklyn. Or a lemon,
an olive. Fruitless, gray trunks
studded with ashen leaves
line the foreign streets.
Just last month, she and Nonna
picked, hulled, and dried almonds
for *torrone* and *amaretti*.

A muted cry wedges her throat.
She prays, *Padre nostro*
that this is a dream, *che sei nei cieli* . . .
that she will open her eyes
to the *centrino all'uncinetto* atop
her nightstand, toss off
lavendered sheets, bound

downstairs, and inhale morning:
*caffè latte e pane di Nonna.*

She wakes to the crowded
apartment and honking horns.
Falters down 21$^{st}$ to PS 247
and Miss Mangano's scowl.

VII

*Maria.* Clara's trilled *r* warms
like sunshine. They skip rope
and clutch like orange blossoms
secret-sharing at the *confetteria*
where Clara's mamma works.
Maria nibbles *frutta martorana:*
*pesca, mela,* and strawberry—
her favorite new word—its seed
dimples perfect. Savors the candied
delights, prolongs the kiss
of almond and natural language.

By mid-November, Papà rents
a basement. She moves
to PS 186, away from Clara.
Sweetness dissolves
like the first dust of snow.

# The Accidental Engineer

"Did you grow vegetables in Chicago?" I ask Dad, while spinning on the rusty swivel stool in his "little house," a narrow, rickety shack where he kept all things horticultural. Over the years, as he saved and stored seeds and transplanted seedlings, I learned much about how to grow things. And about how Dad grew up. He shared glimpses of his childhood—poverty, neglect, and abuse—without a hint of pity. "So many people had it far worse," he said. Even then, I knew he withheld things.

I stand beside him beneath the apple tree, Marlboro dangling from his mouth, as he meticulously cuts away dying and dead branches. "Pruning is essential for new growth," he said. "But you're taking so much off," I replied. He stopped, crouching down to meet my worried gaze, and explained that in winter, trees grow slowly, that he removed fragile and snapped limbs so the tree could use its stored energy on its best branches. "It saves most of that energy for spring, when it wakes up and buds break open, growing stronger and producing more fruit." "More apples, more pies," he winked.

"It's about a tree's structural integrity," he began.

Gardening was his side gig: Dad was an engineer. An aeronautical engineer. An accidental, aeronautical engineer. At NASA. For the son of poor immigrants, who, until age 6, thought Italian the only language that existed, Dad embodied a version of the mythic, vexed American Dream. Throughout high school, he pumped gas and cleaned bathrooms to support his family. Once he graduated—the first in his family to attend school beyond elementary grades—he decided, or maybe was convinced, to take a class or two at the local community college. Working full time, he fit in courses where he could. He liked science, so he started there.

It was the 50s. The Cold War and Space Race were in full force. A couple of NASA engineers visited his metallurgy class and encouraged anyone interested to apply for entry level positions. Dad was and did. He never looked back. Before he knew it, he traded mop for mechanical pencil and began a 43 year career at NASA Ames Research Center in Mountain View. While learning the ropes, NASA supported his earning an engineering degree at San Jose State University, something that as a child seemed as unlikely as the moon landing.

And Dad had chops. He conducted small and large-scale wind tunnel experiments and helped design various planes, including the ground-breaking Tilt-Rotor XV-15. The book he co-authored about the aircraft sits on my desk, next to a photo of him, flashing his signature grin among his legendary tomato plants. As a kid, I beamed when he took me to NASA. Hand in hand, we walked among the aircraft docked in the cold, cavernous wind tunnels. Dad introduced me to his colleagues—groups of men in shirtsleeves and ties—huddled around sleek, futuristic planes that looked like something out of the Jetsons. The planes' details didn't stick, but the pride I felt in my Dad did. I left with a handful of *Property of the US Government* pencils and yellow pads that I used to write stories.

Dad's profession was also a source of great pride and conversation among his friends—bricklayers, gardeners, woodworkers, janitors, and plasters—immigrants, from various parts of the boot, whose families formed our circle of friends. But Dad shied away from the attention. Without an iota of false modesty, he frequently said that his job was "no big deal." He was prouder of his beefsteak tomatoes. And his garden.

Dad's garden was a thing of legend. Every usable square inch of formerly impenetrable clay soil sprouted tomatoes, beans, peas, corn, lettuces, peppers, herbs, and zucchini of all stripes, including—trellised above the other the vegetables—prolific, 2+feet long *cucuzze*, which he affectionately called Sicilian baseball bats, and planted on the insistence of Mom and Nonna. He grew his bounty from seeds, either those he preserved year to year or varieties his friends snuck in from the old country. Returning from a trip to his native Veneto, Dad's friend, Aldo, shared some prized seeds, but kept for himself the parakeet he smuggled in under his hat. On Saturday mornings, our backyard seconded as a horticultural social club: Italian men swapping their garden gems, jokes, and prized contraband.

Within minutes of returning from his day job, Dad donned his other work clothes: older, meticulously ironed collared shirts and chinos—never jeans—lit a Marlboro and surveyed "the south 40": watering here, weeding there, re-tying a branch. He staked his plants with precision that only an engineer could muster (see also chopping onions and hanging pictures). The chicken coop he built, each nail countersunk, could survive an earthquake. And did.

Other kids went to Disneyland; my brother and I went to tomato canning camp. For a week each August, under Nonna's watchful eye, we set up operation in the backyard. To our garden harvest, we added a trunkful of tomatoes that we picked from Central Valley fields before they were tilled back into the soil. Canning Camp yielded over a hundred Mason quarts of *pomodori* that we used year-round. Ironically, Dad didn't like vegetables. He ate them because he did not want to incur the wrath of my health-conscious mom. He joked, "why do you think I grow so many tomatoes—yes, they are technically fruit, but stay with me—more tomatoes means more sauce, means more pasta. Simple arithmetic."

"This is what a real apple looks like," Dad beamed, holding up a striking Gravenstein, red stripes on yellow skin. We did not buy fruit or vegetables. Store-bought produce was expensive, tasteless, and suspiciously shiny. Dad figured, if he were lucky, this elegant striped beauty would find its way into a pie. Simple arithmetic, and the calculus of dessert.

During our "little house" conversations, Dad reflected on how fortune graced us. Because of his job, he and Mom provided my brother and me a better life than he had, one with ample food and security. Medical insurance. From the swivel stool, I learned to devote time to nurturing, to attend to details—shoots on the sides of beans, phases of the moon. To take pride in all work. To strengthen roots—garden and familial—through time, attention, and love.

Over the years, I saw two sides of my dad: a man firmly rooted in soil and routine and someone who found exhilaration on the edges. Dad is lucky to have survived his childhood: calculating physics angles and playing chicken with cars while sledding down steep, icy hills in North Chicago. Building rockets that exploded in tenement alleys. "I nearly lost an eye," he winked. Maybe his harsh boyhood motivated such behavior, or maybe his danger gene was hardwired. At NASA, he sweet-talked his way onto test flights for experimental aircraft. Gleefully, he recounted how, while flying in a prototype 707, the pilot cut the engine, and the plane plummeted to earth before the pilot recovered. "What if the pilot couldn't recover," I worried.

As I prepare to plant my tomatoes, I conjure Dad at my side. *Make sure you have good soil, and you've worked it well. Take care of the seedlings, especially their fragile roots. They are like babies. Transplanting can shock them, so take your time. Be gentle. Dig your planting holes deep enough for strong roots to develop, but not too deep. Make sure the soil is loose so the roots will grow down and out. And water them carefully. Don't flood them. Once tomatoes become established, remember not to water them too much. Their roots will grow and seek water. You want lots of fruit, not just big, full plants. Think of the pasta!*

When his dementia took hold, the last thing Dad let go of was his garden. In late afternoons, moving unsteadily among the rows of plants, he looked down at the soil before turning his gaze upwards towards the heavens. Caught somewhere between.

My dad, Demo Giulianetti, at NASA Ames Research Center, Moffett Field, CA.

# Rupture

*for Dad*

In morning's half-light,
I hike the headlands.
Fog cleaves like regret
then breaks open:
basalted cliffs,
cypress, golden bridge.

Memory catches:
a peach, coral-faced
snaps its stem
and plummets.
I gather the blur
of sweetness and soil.
An unhinged globe
a ruptured world.

My father grafts
scion to rootstock
with engineer's precision
and old-country touch.
Before blossoms open
and his mind seizes.
Before dementia
ruptures our world.

The Pacific's low cry
tracks me back.
Yet I linger
in the slender shadow
before the fall.

# Should I Not Survive the Year

*for Matteo*

Overnight nothing will fit. Shoulders
widen. You outgrow dad's ski boots.

Cherub cheeks hew and lips
shadow. Wet with adulthood.

My son, when the world feels heavy
pause.   Unfurl the map

that boughs inside you. Legended
in New England woods, in expanses

of icy earth, softened by late morning.
Wizard Nonno's curiosity of flight.

Birds and balsa Starfires fluid
Chicago alleys. Coast imagined futures.

Don't be like me, native to worry.
Borrower of trouble. Settling

and ordering before things chance
to unfold.              Or not.

May you catch the updraft
land softly in trampoline meadows.

May you swim in river-long love
messy and exhilarating. It will shake

you to the depths. Its companion,
grief, will plummet you.

Both shape the ground beneath
you, the terrain veining you.

Don't buy into the tortured soul
myth. Steadiness sustains.

Children stretch your capacity
to feel in ways that sound cliché.

But aren't. You only have my word.
The proverbial grain. Assure yourself.

Cannonball into a glossy summer.
Perfect your *carbonara*. Trust your gut.

Keep skateboarding. Keep a journal.
Collect memories in a bucket

below your window: campfires,
black diamond runs, heartbreak.

After you build your next computer,
snow-angel on the grass.

Soon, you'll wing from this place,
chart your own course.

In the darkening dusk
a candle aglow on the sill.

# Santi

*Li morti aprinu l'occhi dei vivi.* \*

*Messina, 1941*

Everyone knew Iacobi killed both sons. Eldest felled
by a shot to the skull, one morning a *montagna*.
He couldn't abide a son in step with *i fascisti*. After
*Papá* paid *il maestro*, I traded pen for hoe,

and, at seven, took to Iacobi's fields. He commanded
us like dogs. I quickly learned to ground my gaze.
A phalanx of mourners, black and bowed,
filed to the estate. Iacobi's face a stone well.

*Il Giudice* appeared, and I waited for the ground swell
the toppled glass. Nothing. Respects paid, rhythm
restored. Dark to dark, taming vines, snapping bud
and cane—anything above the stake. My hands and faith

calloused. "*Vergine Maria Santa,*" the veiled women
incant over Iacobi's youngest. His obituary belies
the truth: Iacobi's boot cracked bone.
The boy's pleas scattered into shivering quiet.

Open doors and windows shepherd souls' departure.
The living remain: eyes peeled by the dead.

---

\* Sicilian proverb, *the dead open the eyes of the living.*

# The Pepper Jar

*for Dad*

Guided by the moon, you germinate
seeds. Transplanting infant plants

well after the final frost. Fostering
them. Withhold water before the harvest

to deepen their flavor, reaping a basket
of red fruit adorned with green hats.

Summer '09: your last labor
of horticultural love.

You lay the nightshades to dry
under the August sun, discarding

those that show softness.
Tending never ends with the harvest.

Two weeks later, their plump, glossy skin
withered as a crone's. Drying animates

their heat and sweetness. With gloves,
glasses, and mask, you remove their stems

and coarsely grind their bodies, filling glass
half pints with flakes that fire sauces and stews.

You warn me not to get too close. I pay
with eyes that burn red and run all night.

This evening, I flavor my *puttanesca*
with a pinch of your red magic, salted

with my tears. Each subtraction multiplies
the loss. You've been gone five years.

I ration what remains, fooling
myself that I'll never hit bottom.

# II. Dwelling

> The desire to go home that is a desire to be whole, to know where you are, to be the point of intersection of all the lines drawn through all the stars, to be the constellation-maker and the center of the world, that center called love.
>
> REBECCA SOLNIT, *STORMING THE GATES OF PARADISE: LANDSCAPES FOR POLITICS*

# What is Left

> *Something to chew on, a dinner*
> *crumb, scrap for Spot (4 down. 3 letters.)*
> *"ORT," my dad said, "what is left."*

Nonna stirs *parmigiano* rinds
into the red ceramic pot, releases
salt and nutty notes into simmering
soup. Removes bay leaves, adds
fresh *basilico* and chunks of stale
bread. She preached *umami* long

before it trended on Food Network.
Reuse before its chicness. I learned
the magic of cheese crusts, to use bulb
and frond for stock, salt and lemon ends
to clean brass. Boiled water from wild
greens flavors *orecchiette*.

Her Singer hummed. As she glided
my dress—a burst of golden daisies—
through the needle plate, I practiced
hand-stitching on floral leavings.
A puckered pouch for my gumball
ruby. Worlds in pieces.

Will lines pared from this poem
find home in others? Or, be swept
to corners like fabric scraps. Forgotten.
I toss espresso grounds below beans
and azaleas. Use her handkerchiefs
to nest photos of the dead.

Into her red pot, I sauté fennel
tops, leek stalks, pepper spines.
Add the *parmigiano*, garden
parsley, and a pinch of dried red
pepper: orts from dad's last batch.
All that remains.

# Lezione: In Cucina

Salt your pasta water well. Never put oil in the pasta water. Rinse the pasta? *Ridicolo!* Where did you hear that? What do Americans know about cooking pasta? Always save the pasta water: *è come l'oro*. You want sauce that sticks to the pasta, no? Only buy Italian brands. What do Americans know about making pasta? *Schiaccia l'aglio*, and don't burn it. Burnt garlic is bitter. And don't use too much. Americans think we add garlic to everything. Save the water you cook *la scarola* in; use it for *minestra*. Save the *parmigiano* rinds; add them to sauces and soups. *Tutto fa brodo.* Save the dry bread crusts for *muddica*. Yesterday's penne? Heat them *bagnomaria*. No, we do not need a microwave.

# Caesura

*for Mom*

With pen not baton     you cipher
in Gregg. Scratch marks on a pad.
Beat time on a Royal Deluxe
while imagining a chorus of flutes.
Pine for the real thing in the Park.

You made slow time through typing
and shorthand. Basted uneven hems,
waxed linoleum in Home Ec. Earned
your commercial diploma and steno
pool future. Destiny marked you early.

Music class, your oasis. After the needle
lifted on Symphony No 3, the room
emptied. You lingered. Mind spinning
in lustrous majors.     Dissonate sharps.
A sudden thunderstorm in high summer.

At the Naumburg Bandshell, you kick
off your heels. Four notes cue suspense
before a soft ascension. Timpani
drums and horns call and respond.
Your hand rings the glossy air.

In dreams you translate Beethoven.
Harken the first violin. The woodwinds.
Direct musicians to hold the *fermata*
until the perfect moment of release.
Your black curls     flying free.

# One of the Good Ones

> *When Mexico sends its people, they're not sending their best . . . They're sending people that have lots of problems . . . They're bringing drugs. They're bringing crime. They're rapists. And some, I assume, are good people.*
>
> DONALD TRUMP, JUNE 16, 2015

Sure, I have problems.
Ten years & four community colleges
to reach the top public university in the US.

I keep my three-year stack of acceptance
letters, responded to with deep regret, tied
with a velvet ribbon, in my oak desk

rescued from South La Brea Avenue
refinished during study breaks
and graphic artist & barista overtiming.

Lacking papers & DACA's thin veil,
I ace the hustle. It's not quite the Resolute
Desk, but it's a desk of my own.

Space for books, laptop, peace
lily. Positioned for maximum light
& a bird's-eye to University Avenue.

Birthplace of my honors thesis:
multi-lingual & cross-disciplinary,
paving my ivy path to an elite

graduate school. I'd say more
but I'm neck-high in grant applications,
cobbling enough cash to avoid

adding this *yes* to the ribboned pile.
Villains you say?    I skirt poverty,
keep my head down. My frequency

tuned to ICE. Wear my mom's amber
ring like a talisman. Ride the bus. Water
my plant.    Criminals? I disappear

your lines with rubber erasers. Draw
the brave: working in shadows, sharing
meals, dancing. You do not define

me. No matter your paralipsis.
Resolute.  Graphite to paper, frame
to frame, I kaleidoscope in black & white.

# Maria Reconceived

I live in the midst of Marias, from the maternal to the eternal. Since my earliest memories, I wanted to be a mother. My Sicilian nonna, Maria Grazia, lost three children before she had my uncle and my mom, Maria Gaetana. My parents broke the trend and made Maria my middle name. Calls to my mom bookend my days: 7AM, on my way from the gym, and 7 PM, as my day slows. Scores of cousins and friends named Maria. A chosen sister, Maria Joaquina.

Maybe my maternal longings rooted over countless Saturday mornings at Nonna's kitchen table, rapt in her memories about motherhood's joys and tragedies. Like a pocket stone, I carried the story of the Allied bombing that leveled a nearby home in *Caropepe*, burying in the rubble a young woman and her newborn. The mother died; the baby beneath her survived. Undoubtedly, numerous weddings, baby showers, and baptisms (see Italian-Catholic social calendar) primed me for a strollering future. Perhaps though, it was something more intrinsic. Hardwired. What I considered my destiny. In graduate school, while developing expanded understandings of womanhood and feminism through studying literature, I simultaneously longed to birth a daughter, another Maria.

When my husband and I decided to start a family, reality body-slammed me. Nature seemed to have had the last laugh. After three years of home remedies, acupuncture, yoga, more exercise, less exercise, more leafy greens, meditation, romantic getaways, a fertility specialist provided a diagnosis: Polycystic Ovary Syndrome (PCOS). The treatment: a regimen of expensive drugs, frequent doctor visits, and a seemingly endless cycle of cautious optimism followed by dashed hopes.

My daily calls to Mom became longer. Nonna fretted that my eyes didn't look right: *"No mi piacciono gli occhi."* Half-jokingly, I dubbed my first fertility med, Clomid, my Sylvia Plath drug; the proverbial bell jar descended. Depression clung like a cold, damp sweater. I felt alien in my skin: dull and heavy, beset by headaches, hirsutism, muscle pain, and acne. I avoided mirrors, eye contact. Hardly ideal baby-making conditions.

My ever-steady New Englander spouse kept things stable and hopeful. He would re-center me when I spiraled towards despair. When he held me, I calmed. Until fear resurfaced and self-loathing's chokehold tightened. I thrive on routine, but sex by charts and clocks dimmed me. However, always the good student, I followed directions, continuing the Clomid, until head-in-an-oven jokes became less funny. Time to try a new medication—more risks, but better pay-offs. I took the gamble.

Quickly, I became a pro at daily self-injecting Follistim, a drug designed to trigger ovulation. Late for a connecting flight at O'Hare and facing the never-ending restroom line, I panicked. Thankfully, my inner Florence Nightingale kicked in: throwing modesty to the wind, I took a syringe from my purse, lifted my sweater, skipped the alcohol swab, and voilá, I made my flight with seconds to spare. Needles unnerve Booker. Yet, always the stalwart, he injected me monthly in a place I could not reach—despite all the yoga.

Marias are ever-present in my life. After the midday Mass crowd cleared, my friend, Gaston, and I would slip into church, light candles, and kneel at the statue of Blessed Mary and baby Jesus. Despite being lapsed Catholics, our candle and Mary habits persisted. (See Immigrant Catholics, Mary, and rituals.) Mary, my favorite in the Catholic pantheon, is more relatable and accessible than the lofty saints and apostles. And being a Maria, familiar. I bargained, pleaded, and whispered the familiar prayer *"Ave Maria, piena di grazia…" Please let me conceive. Please.* A hand on my shoulder. "Ok, pretty, let's go get lunch."

After the doctor called with news that the latest drugs and costly IVF had worked, I made a beeline to Mary. Trembling with elation and fear, I lit a candle. I prayed for Siena Maria. From the moment my pregnancy test came back positive, I knew I was carrying a Maria.

# A letter to Siena Maria

### *20 years later*

The doctor told you to cultivate habits that soothe your anxiety and OCD, mitigate the sadness that thickens as night falls. Quiet your mind as it spirals from one imagined disaster to the next. You've taken up yoga, meditation, journaling, cooking, and gardening, like the Marias before you. You've pulled out paintbrushes, pens, and canvases from the back of your closet. Filled mason jars with water and mixed colors. Painted your nightstand and door. Decorated ceramic pots, filled them with soil, planted peace plants, prayer plants, and succulents. Festooned your room with macramé hangers and diffused the air, lemongrass and lavender.

My sweet, 20-year-old girl, if I could scoop you in my arms and cradle you, rock the bottomless sadness from your body, comb the fear from your long spiral curls, I would. I would.

But I can't. Instead, I crawl into your bed and embrace you, cry with you about the murders in Minneapolis and Atlanta and DC and Oakland. Grieve our forests. Try my best to reassure you that visiting Nonna and social-distancing in her backyard will not risk her health, that Dad—although he takes long bike rides—will be safe, will return home. That I always wear a mask when shopping and hiking.

I can't promise you that our world won't burn, that your fear, anxiety, and sadness will ever fully leave you.

Last week, you collected a pile of magazines, calendars, and greeting cards from the box in the hall closet and spread them out on your bedroom floor. "*Want to collage with me?*" you ask. I have the artistic ability of a pet rock, but collaging is one artistic endeavor that we share, evidenced by years of homemade Valentines. I got down on the floor and picked up a pair of scissors.

I watch you sketch something on your canvas. Cut and plan, affix and position scraps and shapes. Words and worlds. Kaleidoscopic.

Astonished. Speechless. Your collage could hang in a gallery, commanding attention. I'm not sure you believe me.

Assembled in black and white, a naked woman—full hips and round breasts—emerges from a cosmos of color. Pink rose bud areolae and cobalt iris between her thighs.

Regathering, rebirthing yourself.

## If These Trees Could Talk

What would they say?

We leave calls
unanswered, messages
unsent, hairpin
headland curves
and compass

by instinct, until
we unfurl here,
silent
below their Bishop
hats on a day
soft and stilled
by early fall mist.

What would they say
of our wanting
to hold this moment
as trunk holds
branches, needles
hold green.

What would they

      Return
on the full moon.
Bring basket, blanket,
and spirits. Bring
those things unsaid—
stones lading
your pockets
like conifer scales

clinging to protect
their seed.

It's time.

Break through
your coats, turn
down into the earth
and seek clemency
beneath our canopy.

# Pasta con Finocchietto

*per la Festa di San Giuseppe*


From the backseat, eagle-eyed
Nonna demands that Dad stop the car.
*Finocchietto* grows along
the railroad tracks. He cuts the engine.
She cuts tender bunches.

Don't confuse these fronds
with their domesticated farmers'
market bulbed cousins.
*Finocchietti* are wild. Lacy.
Fern-whispy leaves belie
their heartiness. They shoot up
in empty lots, fields,
cracks in the road.

Nonna preps her roadside prize
for its starring role. Sautés
the chopped fronds with *acciughe,
aglio, ed un po' di peperoncino*.
Ladles in *penne* flavored
by vegetable water. Tosses.
Tops with *muddica,* grated
and toasted earlier. In honor
of San Giuseppe, the carpenter,
protector of laborers.
In honor of her homeland.
Of her son, Pino.

*Non é il finocchietto
di montagna,* she laments.

*Le acciughe erano piu saporite*
*l'acqua diversa.*

Displacement
lives on fingertips tipped by knife
cuts. On the unsated tongue. Even
after thirty years and three cities
the body knows what it knows.
What it lacks: Mount Etna silting
stems. The Mediterranean
brining her mouth.

# Nonna's Pasta con Finocchietto

**INGREDIENTS**

A large bunch of clean, tender *finocchietto*
1-2 cloves of garlic, minced
4-5 anchovy filets
1-2 tbsp of *pomodoro passata* or 1 tbsp tomato paste
dried hot pepper
olive oil
1 lb of *penne rigate*
toasted breadcrumbs (*muddica*)

1. Clean and chop the *finocchietto*.

2. Boil the *finocchietto* in salted water until tender, about 10 minutes.

3. Remove from water and set aside to dry. Chop. Retain the cooking water.

4. In a large frying pan, sauté garlic and anchovy in olive oil. Add chopped *finocchietto*, a bit of cooking water, the *pomodoro passata*, thinned with a bit of *finocchietto* water, and a pinch or two of hot pepper—to taste. Season with salt and pepper.

5. Cook *penne* in *finocchietto* water until *al dente*. Ladle the pasta into the frying pan with the other ingredients and toss until the *finocchietto* sauce adheres to the pasta. Add pasta water, as needed. Finish with toasted breadcrumbs (*muddica*).

**NOTES**

\* Do not add grated cheese (*parmigiano, pecorino*, or any other cheese). This dish is not served with cheese.

\* Some people add a bit of green onion when sautéing the garlic and anchovy.

\* Some people add pine nuts (*pignoli*) and/or raisins (*uva passa*) to the *finocchietto* mixture. If using raisins, soak them first in warm water to plump them.

\* If you want to make the more common St. Joseph's Day *Pasta con Le Sarde,* add 7-8 fresh sardines, cleaned, boned, and cut into pieces before adding the cooked, chopped *finocchietto*.

# Beyond Blue

*in memory of Keith B. Stevenson*

EMTs led you down the *Sky Blue's* broken
brick stairs that night of unforgiving wind.

They neither covered you with a blanket
nor used the gurney propped nearby.

You always took those stairs purposefully,
elegantly: Tellason denim, head to Red Wings,

with the promise of a classic car or jazz
tee beneath. Black in gourmet ghetto.

You named it plainly: hostile territory
as we unspooled at the end of Bar César.

Hard to fathom that a month has passed
since you last descended that flight.

Tonight, coral and gold halo the *Sky
Blue.* Later, I'll open a *Chaos Theory*

to dull the gnawing. Was it a slow
bleed? Did you see my last text

about Ernest Gaines? We had Kurt
Elling, front row. Your wine bottle

is gone from the kitchen window.
I never asked you its story.

# Mending World

> *Take it from me, someday we'll all be free.*
> —DONNY HATHAWAY

His words coil
rise     strike.
Centuries-old demon
breaks
bread at my table.

I want to split maple
create a cavern, shutter
our fragile, mending world
from his.
Instead, I walk away.

You remain
in a place well past familiar.
Steadying your swelling throat
you light a verbal footpath
down his crooked alley.

All we have
is a corner of this world
a place to pause, share
a meal, breathe Coltrane
re-member a story.

A jagged corner
our mothers raised
from a golden myth
worked until it bore
almonds, figs, and children's

songs, Sunday lessons
and freedom marches
blessings
before dinner, prayers
for the dying.

And iris:
amethyst hands reaching
skyward
balancing on fragile reeds
throbbing the blues.

# III. Re-Membering

> Perhaps the world will end at the kitchen table, while we are laughing and crying, eating of the last/sweet bite.
>
> JOY HARJO

# Limone

My nephews chase each other around
the century-old tree, like the superheroes
on their tees and caps. I pick a lemon,
cut it in half, then quarters, and bite

it like an apple: pulp, rind, and peel.
I pluck a second. Americans wince
in sympathetic puckers. Some add salt
to pique their sweetness. I prefer them

fresh and sharp like winter's sun. Spiderman
asks for a taste. Sucking the marrow,
juice escaping his small mouth, he extends
a web-shooter and smiles. "More, please."

The boys will learn *acqua e limone*
thwarts colds, settles a stomach, offsets
a heavy meal. They will top the fish
Thor catches with *capperi e limone.*

*Amore,* let's return to Catania,
to the alley bar for *granita di limone
con brioche*, the buttery *tuppo*
shaped like my low-worn bun

that you unpinned every evening.
From our balconied window
we heard them: nectared saffron suns
tripping moonlight, falling to earth.

# Lezione: Sfortuna

No, you cannot have scissors to open your shower gifts. Do you want *sfortuna* to enter your marriage? Next you're going to ask for knives as wedding gifts. Rip the ribbons and paper. Of course you need *bomboniere* for the guests. Five *confetti* for health, happiness, longevity, fertility, and wealth. Always an odd number. You want an unbreakable bond, don't you? Add another plate: we can't have 13 *a tavola. But it's an odd number. And 13 people are coming for dinner.* Add a plate; don't argue. And, don't cross the silverware.

# Making Space

Some days, it's the little things.
Others
           saucer sized gold
hoops and 4-inch fuchsia
heels you've had no business
wearing for decades.

You paint your entryway *Ionian
Blue*. Festoon it with Pothos
Laceleaf and Crown-of-Thorns.

You exhume the blood-red garnet
ring he gave you
the one you buried in the back
of the miscellaneous drawer—behind
used birthday candles, matchbooks
and packets of *Fresh Flower
Food* tossed into mixed bouquets—
the ring you never wore.
The one he presented cradled in velvet
with fanfare like he was gifting
you keys to the fucking kingdom.

Through her loupe, the jeweler
remarks the setting is a bit dated.
You think *more than you know.*
Request she remake it—a single
pendant.    Free floating.
An emancipated pomegranate eye
to hang on your heirloom chain
alongside your mom's slender
heart and her mom's pearl. You hear
he's culture-vulturing in Santa Fe.
You hope a whip scorpion finds him.

But enough of that.
You have a bench to polish.
The ceiling to paint *starlight*.
Votives to place in the nook
near the front door.

You arrange freshly cut peonies.
Showy carnelian petals bursting
from rose solitaire centers.
Their citrus-sweetness incenses
the vestibule, to which only you hold
the key     and few are granted entry.

# Salvation: A Blues

> *I can take you there if you want to go.*
> *Let's make a kingdom. Let's make a city of bones.*
>
> AUNT ESTER, GEM OF THE OCEAN

*Citizen* begs emancipation
like a fugitive pleads bread.
Aunt Ester takes his parlor
confession, threading testaments,
seabeds, and underground railroads:
two pennies for his penance.

Bill of sale becomes boat
a-sail. She christens *Gem of the Ocean*
to pilot him through fevered
crossings, beyond depth charts
to fiery tongues, to the city of bones.
Starboard to salvation.

A paper compasses: truer
than any amendment, stronger
than Caesar's grip
heavier than a bucket of nails.
Like Solly's walking stick—62 notches,
62 saved—steady for 800 ahead.

*The world is not easy.*
As you find the road,
remember the North Star
homespun on a clothesline.
Hope hidden in plain sight
swaying under unraveling sun.

# Sheltering with Sunflowers

Lush branches and serrated
heart-shaped leaves tower.
But not a single golden flower.

The promise to shield peppers,
tomatoes, lettuce chimeric
like most things these days:
our anniversary trip. Jazz
jamming a crowded club.

As their stalks stretch skyward
I zoom, fret, shelter. Will buds
to open, to lantern the days:
the growing dread
the growing dead.

Beyond the crawl of morning
glories, I see them: two stars
emerging from thick green.
The beginning of a prayer.
Patience's reward.

Their young faces gaze east
at first light, greet and track
the sun, then turn and inch
back west. Entice late heat
before their overnight return.

Petals sprout from their saffron
faces. Weighty, proud, the stalks
cease sun tracking. Claim their place.
Hail bees to feast. Majestic
like the queen of wands.

Coruscating. They bank time before the fall. The space between effort and surrender.

# Finding Home

When the *Frappato* arrives,
I land in your mom's kitchen.
Days from my mom's
yet around-the-corner
familiar: stock pot simmers,
ceiling fan whirls, bucket
full of peaches—rosy and dusty—
ready to peel.

She ladles boiling, fragrant
preserves—tree sweet
with a whisper of lemon—
into Mason half-pints
leaving ample headspace.
Circles rims with a damp towel
seals with a wide, silver band.
A summer wedding.

Under the almond tree, Nonna
shells peas, teaches me to tug
stems backwards, unzip pods.
Small, green pearls cascade
into a bowl at her feet. My hands
fumble, move at half speed. I sneak
a pearl here and there: spring
bursts sugar in my mouth.

You and I ferry to Smögen's coast,
fish at first light. Share Tomales
Bay fried oysters. Zigzag
through Catania sidestreets; feast
on *arancini* and *bucatini con sarde*.
Land in a Harlem room

as your mom prepares love letters
in verdant greens.

Half a mile from home, we travel
half a century: late peaches, folded
apron, cast iron. Cross borders
and seas to gather at familiar
tables. Hand to mouth, an *Amaro*
assuages mourning. We cup
the past in our palms.
Fingers folded for grace.

# Caponata

When *caponata* is cooking, the kitchen fills with the unmistakable sensory punch of *agrodolce*, a sauce/condiment/preparation method that reduces sour and sweet ingredients to sticky deliciousness. A staple of many Sicilian dishes, *agrodolce* has roots in the island's Arab influence. The term *caponata* first appears in print in a 1759 etymological text printed in Messina where it is defined as a *"dish made up of various things."*

*Caponata* begins with the peeling and chopping of its star ingredient: eggplant. Per my mom and nonna's method, eggplant chunks are generously salted, placed in a colander, and weighted down with a plate, to release residual bitterness and excess moisture. As it is frying, the spongy eggplant absorbs the flavors of other ingredients—olives, capers, onions, peppers, celery, and tomatoes—and becomes coated with zesty, caramelized *agrodolce*. Mouthwatering. A simple preparation with complex flavors.

*Caponata*, like most Sicilian dishes, varies from region to region, town to town, family to family. It is best enjoyed on crusty bread with a crisp, minerally Sicilian white wine such as an *Etna Bianco* or a citrusy *Grillo*. It can also accompany grilled, baked, or pan-fried chicken or fish.

# My family's Caponata

INGREDIENTS

3 eggplants, choose those with the fewest seeds
2 green peppers, charred, peeled, and sliced
½ onion, chopped
¾ C of celery, chopped and par-cooked
1 C or so of green olives that have been par-boiled and chopped roughly
A handful of capers
A bit of crushed tomato or *passata*
Sugar
Vinegar, preferably homemade

1. Peel and cube the eggplant, salt generously. Place in a colander and top with a weight, such as a heavy plate. This removes bitterness and excess liquid from the eggplant.

2. About an hour later, after the water has drained out, rinse the eggplant well. Dry thoroughly.

3. In a large frying pan, heat olive oil and fry the eggplant. Do not crowd it; if need be, fry in batches, until the eggplant is browned. (Or, if you prefer, sprinkle the eggplant generously with oil and bake at 400 degrees until brown). Remove from pan.

4. Next, sauté the onion until soft. Add the eggplant, peppers, and celery and sauté for a few minutes. Add the tomato and simmer until it has reduced to a saucy consistency.

5. Add capers and olives. Season with salt and pepper. Simmer for about 10 minutes on medium heat.

6. Make space in the pan for the sugar and add it. Then, pour the vinegar over the sugar. Stir so that the sugar and vinegar combine and carmelize. Stir through other ingredients. Simmer for a few more minutes.

7. Taste for salt, pepper, sugar, and vinegar.

8. Add some chopped fresh basil before serving. Enjoy!

> Other versions of *caponata* add sultanas, raisins, pine nuts, honey instead of sugar, and fresh parsley rather than basil.

# How to Drink Coffee Like an Italian: A Guide

*Caffè*
is sacred.
Drinking it is a spiritual experience.
*Caffè* is espresso. Order *un caffè, per favore.*
Drink your *caffè* standing or leaning against a bar.
Drink it in three or four sips. Don't dawdle.
Add sugar or enjoy it straight. Give it a quick stir
with the small spoon provided by the barista.
Don't tote it in stickered metal carafes, mugs, or disposable cups.
Do not drink while driving, walking, or shopping.
Drink *caffè* throughout the day.
At dawn. Midmorning.
Post lunch or dinner.
Before bed.
*Un caffè* aids digestion.
*Espresso*, not EXpresso.
From *esprimere* (verb), to press out.
*Latte* means milk. Order a *latte*,
and you will get a glass of milk.
If you want warm milk with your *caffè*, order a *caffè latte.*
Do not expect pumpkin spice or caramel swirl.
Or order a *cappuccino*: a shot of *caffè* topped
with frothed milk, served in a small cup.
Do not request a short, tall, or grande.
*Caffè latte* and *cappuccino* are morning drinks.
Post morning, stick with *caffè* or *caffè macchiato.*
Suspend your disbelief and your *caffè*:
Order *caffè sospeso*, like the Neapolitans.
Pay for two; drink one.
Leave the other for a stranger to enjoy.
*Due caffè, per favore.*

# Red, White, and Boiled

*Boiled and mashed.* I recite this refrain to myself before the Christmas meal is served, as I have for 20+ years of biennial holiday visits with my husband's family. I am Italian. My mom and dad have their roots in the boot. My husband and his family are not: New Englanders for centuries, as the cemetery alongside their 250-year-old house attests. Stoic, hardy Northern European stock, with a penchant for things snowy, plaid, and boiled. I boil pasta: that's about it. For Italians, food is serious business. Holiday food, nothing short of sacred.

Like most things in my in-laws' home, the dining table dates back to Emerson. Nine white plates, nine red napkins. Christmas tablecloth pressed. The good glasses, carefully removed from their boxes and wiped spotless, positioned precisely over the knives. The showpiece turkey, carved in the kitchen: white meat on one plate, dark on the other. Brown gravy afloat in its boat. Cranberry crimson in a crystal round. And four clear bowls holding things boiled, mashed, buttered, and salted: sweet potatoes, white potatoes, and winter squash. The only items to escape the mash are pearl onions. A bowl of anemic eyeballs. One Christmas Eve, I sautéed pearl onions with olive oil, thyme, and balsamic vinegar, caramelized them to draw out their sweetness, and drizzled the syrupy simmer liquid over the bronzed orbs. They were met—in atypical New England fashion—with effusive praise. Not a bronze veil remained. The next day, a bowl of boiled eyeballs circulated the Christmas table. Tradition wins.

As I fill my plate with scoops of boiled and mashed, I imagine Christmas dinner 3000 miles away in California. Lasagna will be *il primo.* For Italians, no holiday meal—even Thanksgiving, the most American of them all—is complete without pasta: *lasagna, ravioli, fettuccine Bolognese, cannelloni.* Nor without a fried vegetable—artichoke hearts, *cardoni, fior di zucca*—fluffy treasures nestled in golden *pastella*. Nonna added the right amount of water—she never measured—to flour to make a perfect batter. I cannot duplicate it. Ignoring her warnings and burning my tongue, I snagged a fried treat, moments after she placed it on a paper-towel lined tray on the washing machine next to the downstairs stove. (No self-respecting Italian home has one stove.) But the burn was worth it. Nothing beats the taste and texture of fresh-from-the-oil *fior di zucca*. Morsels of bliss.

Swallowing a forkful of mashed potatoes, I think, with a few more ingredients, some rolling, cutting, and fork creasing, we could be eating gnocchi. Such moments highlight how Italian I am, how food structures my daily thoughts and rhythms. No sooner do I finish breakfast that I plan dinner. I grow herbs year-round. Italian meals extend for hours; we don't just eat, we talk about the food we're eating: its preparation, regional variations, its bastardization by Americans. Chicken and pineapple on pizza? *Che schifo!*

Nonna's kitchen was my first classroom. As we trimmed flat beans and kneaded dough at the table, I learned about Sicily—its history, geography, and cultures. Nonna recounted stories of wars, her journey to America, and how loss framed her life: three babies buried, and, soon after arriving stateside, my grandfather's death. Cooking for and sharing food with her family was an act of love. A testament to survival.

My mother-in-law has come to understand that food is hard-wired in my DNA. A few years back, she gave me free reign for Christmas Eve dinner (see aforementioned caramelized onions). For Italians, Christmas Eve, *la vigilia,* is a feast of fish—traditionally seven. Thankfully, *baccalà* is available in New Hampshire. It is Atlantic cod, after all. I have treated—or possibly subjected—the Anglo side of my family to various preparations: grilled with rosemary, transported from California, stewed with briny olives and capers, and fried with *ceci* beans, if available. My attempt to re-create through food a semblance of home. My mother-in-law tells me, she ate dried cod growing up. "We boiled it in white sauce." Of course, they did.

Jokes about American white sauce aside, reliance on inexpensive, preserved products is cross-cultural. As is the "waste-not" axiom. Like my family, my husband's struggled. I learned how they grew and pickled their own vegetables, ran a summer vegetable stand, hunted, and made maple syrup to make ends meet. A reality that resonates with Nonna's stories of food scarcity, of families foraging through harvested wheat fields for remnants of stray grain.

My *linguine ai gamberi* has become a perennial *vigilia* favorite with the New Englanders. While chopping garlic and cleaning shrimp, I chide myself for not adding garden parsley to the bundle of rosemary, dried hot pepper, espresso beans, and *Panettone* I pack for the trip East. Once, upon request, I made tiramisù. After asking for *mascarpone* at the local market, I was met with a quizzical look: "mozzarella?" Whipped ricotta and heavy cream proved a workable substitute. Two years later, I found *mascarpone* in the dairy case. Progress. *Panettone,* however, remains a solitary pleasure.

When in New Hampshire, I miss 25+ person California holiday dinners, with their cacophony of Italian, Sicilian, and English, raucous political discussion, free-flowing wine, long-into-the-night card games, and talk about food. The food; always the food. I have, however, grown to treasure much about New England Christmas. A freshly cut balsam fir aglow with homemade ornaments; silent snow falling, lit only by the moon and candles in the windows. Pure magic. And Christmas pies. No one makes pies like my mother-in-law.

# Within a World so Heavenly

> *Go home and write / a page tonight. / And let that*
> *page come out of you - / Then, it will be true.*
> LANGSTON HUGHES

Take the "A" train to 125$^{th}$
walk, finger-laced, past the Apollo
down Lenox to Sylvia's. Our only
plan is no plan. You braille

my spine, in an alley straight
out of Jacob Lawrence: cast-iron
fire escapes, street-car tracks, jump
rope. Reds and yellows

frame the *Beauty Shoppe*. After
hours at the Schomburg, you lure
with promises of cornbread
and Rooster Punch. Sway

to Bluenote time. Entwined,
lazing to the hum outside
our brownstone, we rise for church:
Langston's E 127th rowhouse

where he penned rivers and seas.
Catch the Dance Theatre, catch
our breath. At Abyssinian Baptist,
stained glass reverberates Powell

preaching. Midnight autumn breeze
wraps even closer, encircles
us in Strayhorn, streetsong, starlight.
This night divine.

# Open Door

*for Carolyn Mitchell*

The day the dam broke inside of me,
I climbed the steps of St. Joseph's Hall
crossed your portal, found sanctuary.

I returned.     You led me to Lorde,
Sarton, and Morrison. Madwomen
in attics and daughters searching

their mothers' gardens. Finding their own.
Your lectures, inspired hymns. Eyes
closed, thumb and index circling, galaxies

poured from you. I filled notebooks, hungry
for starlit paths. I dove into the wreck;
you held the ladder.

My courage gathered.     *Come in.*
Your embrace unhinged me.
I wish I could tell you.

But you would neither understand
nor remember. Dementia's tempest
roared. Silenced you.     Journals

and letters unread.     Rigid hands
unable to pen a single word.
On my desk, the book you gifted

me, inscribed in your filigreed
script: *who sees herself as protégé—
but is truly mentor.*

A student waits at my door.

# Notes

The first line of the opening poem comes from Jericho Brown's "Duplex."

Brynn Saito's "Daughter" sparked "Letter to My Son Should I Not Survive the Year."

*Gregg* is a form of shorthand invented in the late 19C. It is the most popular form of shorthand in the US and was taught to women in high school and vocational schools to prepare them for careers as secretaries and stenographers.

*Chaos Theory* is a lush red blend made by Brown Estate Vineyards, Napa Valley. "Over the years this proprietary red has become a shape-shifter, each vintage its own unique blend. Such is our journey through the world of wine — a constant adventure that reminds us year in and year out that no matter how random or chaotic things may seem, amidst the mayhem there is reason, if not always rhyme." (Brown Estate website)

*Bagnomaria* means heating in a water bath. The food to be heated is placed in a bowl inside a pot of water simmering on the stovetop. Heat is transmitted gently, and the food cooks or re-heats slowly. Synonymous with the French *Bain-Marie*.

*Bomboniere* are favors given out for special events. Like most things Italian, *bomboniere* are steeped in tradition and superstition. They are a gesture of thanks. *Confetti*, sugared almonds, are presented to wedding guests in decorative bags, boxes, or other containers. *Five confetti* are given to represent happiness, health, longevity, fertility, and wealth for a married couple.

"Gem of the Ocean" was inspired by a 2016 production of August Wilson's *Gem of the Ocean* at the Marin Theatre Company.

Gratitude to my daughter, Siena Bense, for drawing the Moka pot, and Marithza Quiroz for her graphic artist magic—adding my words to the image.

# Acknowledgements

I am grateful to the following journals in which these poems and essays first appeared. Certain titles and versions have been altered.

"Kneading" and "Within a World so Heavenly" *Tule Review.*
"Should I Not Survive the Year" *Stephen A. DiBiase Poetry Prize*
"The Pepper Jar" *Streetlight Magazine*
"A Temporary Matter" and "Salvation: A Blue*" Brilliant Corners*
"Rupture" *riverbabble*
"Santi" *Feile-Festa*
"Maria Reconceived" and "A Letter to Siena Maria" *HerStry*
"Limone" *Italian Americana*
"Finding Home" *CALYX*

I am deeply grateful and indebted to many. Carolyn Mitchell, teacher and mentor, nurtured my love of literature and lit a new way for me to walk this world. For his encouragement, counsel, and friendship, I thank Indigo Moor. I birthed a number of these pieces in Liz Rosner's magic living room, among generous, nurturing writers. Warm thanks to Liz and the guardians of the magic. My nephews, Marco and Diego, keep me on my aged toes. To Gaston Alonso, Gonzalo Arrizon, Becky Bense, Carol Bense, Haydet Giulianetti, Liz Keithley, Dorothy Lazard, Kyle Livie, Judy Lookabill, Pauly Pagenhart, Michelle Perata, Rama Ramachandran, María Villaseñor, Beth Williams, how fortunate I am to have you in my life. To my students, who are also my teachers. To those on the other side: my dad who visits in my dreams, Uncle Joe, Nonna Grazia, Keith Stevenson (Giacomo cocktails and *this, that, & the other* conversation await), and to the generations before me whose stories, whispers, and courage footpathed me here. To Bordighera Press for giving this book a home.

Last and foremost. To my parents, whose immeasurable love and unfailing support sustain me. From them, I learned the value of community. Because of them, I carry home wherever I go. To my brother, David, who I am fortunate to also call friend, for his love, generosity, and wit. And, to my heart's home: Booker, Siena, and Matteo. Always.

# About the Author

LUISA MARIA GIULIANETTI is Bay Area born and bred, the daughter of Italian parents. Her first languages were Italian and Sicilian, and the kitchen table—where friends and family gathered to share food and stories—her first classroom.

She is published in *Brilliant Corners*, *CALYX*, *Feile-Festa*, *HerStry*, *Italian Americana*, *Motherscope*, *Ploughshares*, *Rattle*, *Tule Review*, and *VIA*. For her, food is sacred: rooted, like writing, in history, lore, storytelling. And love. Luisa directs student programs and teaches at UC Berkeley. *Agrodolce* is her first collection.

## *VIA* FOLIOS
*A refereed book series dedicated to the culture of Italians and Italian Americans.*

ANGELO ZEOLLA. *The Bronx Unbound ovvero i versi bronxesi.* Vol. 162. Poetry.
NICHOLAS A. DiCHARIO. *Giovanni's Tree.* Vol. 161. Literature.
ADELE ANNESI. *What She Takes Away.* Vol. 160. Novel.
ANNIE RACHELE LANZILLOTTO. *Whaddyacall the Wind?.* Vol. 159. Memoir.
JULIA LISELLA. *Our Lively Kingdom.* Vol. 158. Poetry.
MARK CIABATTARI. *When the Mask Slips.* Vol. 157. Novel.
JENNIFER MARTELLI. *The Queen of Queens.* Vol. 156. Poetry.
TONY TADDEI. *The Sons of the Santorelli.* Vol. 155. Literature.
FRANCO RICCI. *Preston Street • Corso Italias.* Vol. 154. History.
MIKE FIORITO. *The Hated Ones.* Vol. 153. Literature.
PATRICIA DUNN. *Last Stop on the 6.* Vol. 152. Novel.
WILLIAM BOELHOWER. *Immigrant Autobiography.* Vol. 151. Literary Criticism.
MARC DIPAOLO. *Fake Italian.* Vol. 150. Literature.
GAIL REITANO. *Italian Love Cake.* Vol. 149. Novel.
VINCENT PANELLA. *Sicilian Dreams.* Vol. 148. Novel.
MARK CIABATTARI. *The Literal Truth: Rizzoli Dreams of Eating the Apple of Earthly Delights.* Vol. 147. Novel.
MARK CIABATTARI. *Dreams of An Imaginary New Yorker Named Rizzoli.* Vol. 146. Novel.
LAURETTE FOLK. *The End of Aphrodite.* Vol. 145. Novel.
ANNA CITRINO. *A Space Between.* Vol. 144. Poetry
MARIA FAMÀ. *The Good for the Good.* Vol. 143. Poetry.
ROSEMARY CAPPELLO. *Wonderful Disaster.* Vol. 142. Poetry.
B. AMORE. *Journeys on the Wheel.* Vol. 141. Poetry.
ALDO PALAZZESCHI. *The Manifestos of Aldo Palazzeschi.* Vol 140. Literature.
ROSS TALARICO. *The Reckoning.* Vol 139. Poetry.
MICHELLE REALE. *Season of Subtraction.* Vol 138. Poetry.
MARISA FRASCA. *Wild Fennel.* Vol 137. Poetry.
RITA ESPOSITO WATSON. *Italian Kisses.* Vol. 136. Memoir.
SARA FRUNER. *Bitter Bites from Sugar Hills.* Vol. 135. Poetry.
KATHY CURTO. *Not for Nothing.* Vol. 134. Memoir.
JENNIFER MARTELLI. *My Tarantella.* Vol. 133. Poetry.
MARIA TERRONE. *At Home in the New World.* Vol. 132. Essays.
GIL FAGIANI. *Missing Madonnas.* Vol. 131. Poetry.
LEWIS TURCO. *The Sonnetarium.* Vol. 130. Poetry.
JOE AMATO. *Samuel Taylor's Hollywood Adventure.* Vol. 129. Novel.
BEA TUSIANI. *Con Amore.* Vol. 128. Memoir.
MARIA GIURA. *What My Father Taught Me.* Vol. 127. Poetry.
STANISLAO PUGLIESE. *A Century of Sinatra.* Vol. 126. Popular Culture.
TONY ARDIZZONE. *The Arab's Ox.* Vol. 125. Novel.
PHYLLIS CAPELLO. *Packs Small Plays Big.* Vol. 124. Literature.
FRED GARDAPHÉ. *Read 'em and Reap.* Vol. 123. Criticism.
JOSEPH A. AMATO. *Diagnostics.* Vol 122. Literature.

DENNIS BARONE. *Second Thoughts.* Vol 121. Poetry.
OLIVIA K. CERRONE. *The Hunger Saint.* Vol 120. Novella.
GARIBLADI M. LAPOLLA. *Miss Rollins in Love.* Vol 119. Novel.
JOSEPH TUSIANI. *A Clarion Call.* Vol 118. Poetry.
JOSEPH A. AMATO. *My Three Sicilies.* Vol 117. Poetry & Prose.
MARGHERITA COSTA. *Voice of a Virtuosa and Coutesan.* Vol 116. Poetry.
NICOLE SANTALUCIA. *Because I Did Not Die.* Vol 115. Poetry.
MARK CIABATTARI. *Preludes to History.* Vol 114. Poetry.
HELEN BAROLINI. *Visits.* Vol 113. Novel.
ERNESTO LIVORNI. *The Fathers' America.* Vol 112. Poetry.
MARIO B. MIGNONE. *The Story of My People.* Vol 111. Non-fiction.
GEORGE GUIDA. *The Sleeping Gulf.* Vol 110. Poetry.
JOEY NICOLETTI. *Reverse Graffiti.* Vol 109. Poetry.
GIOSE RIMANELLI. *Il mestiere del furbo.* Vol 108. Criticism.
LEWIS TURCO. *The Hero Enkidu.* Vol 107. Poetry.
AL TACCONELLI. *Perhaps Fly.* Vol 106. Poetry.
RACHEL GUIDO DEVRIES. *A Woman Unknown in Her Bones.* Vol 105. Poetry.
BERNARD BRUNO. *A Tear and a Tear in My Heart.* Vol 104. Non-fiction.
FELIX STEFANILE. *Songs of the Sparrow.* Vol 103. Poetry.
FRANK POLIZZI. *A New Life with Bianca.* Vol 102. Poetry.
GIL FAGIANI. *Stone Walls.* Vol 101. Poetry.
LOUISE DESALVO. *Casting Off.* Vol 100. Fiction.
MARY JO BONA. *I Stop Waiting for You.* Vol 99. Poetry.
RACHEL GUIDO DEVRIES. *Stati zitt, Josie.* Vol 98. Children's Literature. $8
GRACE CAVALIERI. *The Mandate of Heaven.* Vol 97. Poetry.
MARISA FRASCA. *Via incanto.* Vol 96. Poetry.
DOUGLAS GLADSTONE. *Carving a Niche for Himself.* Vol 95. History.
MARIA TERRONE. *Eye to Eye.* Vol 94. Poetry.
CONSTANCE SANCETTA. *Here in Cerchio.* Vol 93. Local History.
MARIA MAZZIOTTI GILLAN. *Ancestors' Song.* Vol 92. Poetry.
MICHAEL PARENTI. *Waiting for Yesterday: Pages from a Street Kid's Life.* Vol 90. Memoir.
ANNIE LANZILLOTTO. *Schistsong.* Vol 89. Poetry.
EMANUEL DI PASQUALE. *Love Lines.* Vol 88. Poetry.
CAROSONE & LOGIUDICE. *Our Naked Lives.* Vol 87. Essays.
JAMES PERICONI. *Strangers in a Strange Land: A Survey of Italian-Language American Books.* Vol 86. Book History.
DANIELA GIOSEFFI. *Escaping La Vita Della Cucina.* Vol 85. Essays.
MARIA FAMÀ. *Mystics in the Family.* Vol 84. Poetry.
ROSSANA DEL ZIO. *From Bread and Tomatoes to Zuppa di Pesce "Ciambotto".* Vol. 83. Memoir.
LORENZO DELBOCA. *Polentoni.* Vol 82. Italian Studies.
SAMUEL GHELLI. *A Reference Grammar.* Vol 81. Italian Language.
ROSS TALARICO. *Sled Run.* Vol 80. Fiction.
FRED MISURELLA. *Only Sons.* Vol 79. Fiction.
FRANK LENTRICCHIA. *The Portable Lentricchia.* Vol 78. Fiction.

RICHARD VETERE. *The Other Colors in a Snow Storm*. Vol 77. Poetry.
GARIBALDI LAPOLLA. *Fire in the Flesh*. Vol 76 Fiction & Criticism.
GEORGE GUIDA. *The Pope Stories*. Vol 75 Prose.
ROBERT VISCUSI. *Ellis Island*. Vol 74. Poetry.
ELENA GIANINI BELOTTI. *The Bitter Taste of Strangers Bread*. Vol 73. Fiction.
PINO APRILE. *Terroni*. Vol 72. Italian Studies.
EMANUEL DI PASQUALE. *Harvest*. Vol 71. Poetry.
ROBERT ZWEIG. *Return to Naples*. Vol 70. Memoir.
AIROS & CAPPELLI. *Guido*. Vol 69. Italian/American Studies.
FRED GARDAPHÉ. *Moustache Pete is Dead! Long Live Moustache Pete!*. Vol 67. Literature/Oral History.
PAOLO RUFFILLI. *Dark Room/Camera oscura*. Vol 66. Poetry.
HELEN BAROLINI. *Crossing the Alps*. Vol 65. Fiction.
COSMO FERRARA. *Profiles of Italian Americans*. Vol 64. Italian Americana.
GIL FAGIANI. *Chianti in Connecticut*. Vol 63. Poetry.
BASSETTI & D'ACQUINO. *Italic Lessons*. Vol 62. Italian/American Studies.
CAVALIERI & PASCARELLI, Eds. *The Poet's Cookbook*. Vol 61. Poetry/Recipes.
EMANUEL DI PASQUALE. *Siciliana*. Vol 60. Poetry.
NATALIA COSTA, Ed. *Bufalini*. Vol 59. Poetry.
RICHARD VETERE. *Baroque*. Vol 58. Fiction.
LEWIS TURCO. *La Famiglia/The Family*. Vol 57. Memoir.
NICK JAMES MILETI. *The Unscrupulous*. Vol 56. Humanities.
BASSETTI. ACCOLLA. D'AQUINO. *Italici: An Encounter with Piero Bassetti*. Vol 55. Italian Studies.
GIOSE RIMANELLI. *The Three-legged One*. Vol 54. Fiction.
CHARLES KLOPP. *Bele Antiche Stòrie*. Vol 53. Criticism.
JOSEPH RICAPITO. *Second Wave*. Vol 52. Poetry.
GARY MORMINO. *Italians in Florida*. Vol 51. History.
GIANFRANCO ANGELUCCI. *Federico F*. Vol 50. Fiction.
ANTHONY VALERIO. *The Little Sailor*. Vol 49. Memoir.
ROSS TALARICO. *The Reptilian Interludes*. Vol 48. Poetry.
RACHEL GUIDO DE VRIES. *Teeny Tiny Tino's Fishing Story*. Vol 47. Children's Literature.
EMANUEL DI PASQUALE. *Writing Anew*. Vol 46. Poetry.
MARIA FAMÀ. *Looking For Cover*. Vol 45. Poetry.
ANTHONY VALERIO. *Toni Cade Bambara's One Sicilian Night*. Vol 44. Poetry.
EMANUEL CARNEVALI. *Furnished Rooms*. Vol 43. Poetry.
BRENT ADKINS. et al., Ed. *Shifting Borders. Negotiating Places*. Vol 42. Conference.
GEORGE GUIDA. *Low Italian*. Vol 41. Poetry.
GARDAPHÈ, GIORDANO, TAMBURRI. *Introducing Italian Americana*. Vol 40. Italian/American Studies.
DANIELA GIOSEFFI. *Blood Autumn/Autunno di sangue*. Vol 39. Poetry.
FRED MISURELLA. *Lies to Live By*. Vol 38. Stories.
STEVEN BELLUSCIO. *Constructing a Bibliography*. Vol 37. Italian Americana.
ANTHONY JULIAN TAMBURRI, Ed. *Italian Cultural Studies 2002*. Vol 36. Essays.

BEA TUSIANI. *con amore*. Vol 35. Memoir.
FLAVIA BRIZIO-SKOV, Ed. *Reconstructing Societies in the Aftermath of War.*
  Vol 34. History.
TAMBURRI. et al., Eds. *Italian Cultural Studies 2001*. Vol 33. Essays.
ELIZABETH G. MESSINA, Ed. *In Our Own Voices.*
  Vol 32. Italian/American Studies.
STANISLAO G. PUGLIESE. *Desperate Inscriptions*. Vol 31. History.
HOSTERT & TAMBURRI, Eds. *Screening Ethnicity.*
  Vol 30. Italian/American Culture.
G. PARATI & B. LAWTON, Eds. *Italian Cultural Studies*. Vol 29. Essays.
HELEN BAROLINI. *More Italian Hours*. Vol 28. Fiction.
FRANCO NASI, Ed. *Intorno alla Via Emilia*. Vol 27. Culture.
ARTHUR L. CLEMENTS. *The Book of Madness & Love*. Vol 26. Poetry.
JOHN CASEY, et al. *Imagining Humanity*. Vol 25. Interdisciplinary Studies.
ROBERT LIMA. *Sardinia/Sardegna*. Vol 24. Poetry.
DANIELA GIOSEFFI. *Going On*. Vol 23. Poetry.
ROSS TALARICO. *The Journey Home*. Vol 22. Poetry.
EMANUEL DI PASQUALE. *The Silver Lake Love Poems*. Vol 21. Poetry.
JOSEPH TUSIANI. *Ethnicity*. Vol 20. Poetry.
JENNIFER LAGIER. *Second Class Citizen*. Vol 19. Poetry.
FELIX STEFANILE. *The Country of Absence*. Vol 18. Poetry.
PHILIP CANNISTRARO. *Blackshirts*. Vol 17. History.
LUIGI RUSTICHELLI, Ed. *Seminario sul racconto*. Vol 16. Narrative.
LEWIS TURCO. *Shaking the Family Tree*. Vol 15. Memoirs.
LUIGI RUSTICHELLI, Ed. *Seminario sulla drammaturgia.*
  Vol 14. Theater/Essays.
FRED GARDAPHÈ. *Moustache Pete is Dead! Long Live Moustache Pete!.*
  Vol 13. Oral Literature.
JONE GAILLARD CORSI. *Il libretto d'autore. 1860 - 1930*. Vol 12. Criticism.
HELEN BAROLINI. *Chiaroscuro: Essays of Identity*. Vol 11. Essays.
PICARAZZI & FEINSTEIN, Eds. *An African Harlequin in Milan.*
  Vol 10. Theater/Essays.
JOSEPH RICAPITO. *Florentine Streets & Other Poems*. Vol 9. Poetry.
FRED MISURELLA. *Short Time*. Vol 8. Novella.
NED CONDINI. *Quartettsatz*. Vol 7. Poetry.
ANTHONY JULIAN TAMBURRI, Ed. *Fuori: Essays by Italian/American*
  *Lesbiansand Gays*. Vol 6. Essays.
ANTONIO GRAMSCI. P. Verdicchio. Trans. & Intro. *The Southern Question.*
  Vol 5. Social Criticism.
DANIELA GIOSEFFI. *Word Wounds & Water Flowers*. Vol 4. Poetry. $8
WILEY FEINSTEIN. *Humility's Deceit: Calvino Reading Ariosto Reading Calvino.*
  Vol 3. Criticism.
PAOLO A. GIORDANO, Ed. *Joseph Tusiani: Poet. Translator. Humanist.*
  Vol 2. Criticism.
ROBERT VISCUSI. *Oration Upon the Most Recent Death of Christopher Columbus.*
  Vol 1. Poetry.

www.ingramcontent.com/pod-product-compliance
Lightning Source LLC
Chambersburg PA
CBHW022118090426
42743CB00008B/902